Introduction

Welcome to "Cryptocurrency Simplified: A Beginner's Guide to Digital Wealth." If you've found your way to this book, chances are you're intrigued by the noise around cryptocurrencies and digital assets and want to understand what it's all about. Maybe you've heard stories of people becoming overnight millionaires through Bitcoin, or maybe you're simply fascinated by this revolutionary technology that is disrupting our traditional financial systems.

In this book, we will be your guide, breaking down complex jargon into simple terms and concepts. You don't need a degree in computer science or finance to understand this book – we've designed it specifically for beginners just like you.

So, why is understanding cryptocurrency important?

Well, we are on the brink of a new digital revolution. Cryptocurrency is not just another buzzword. It's the future of finance, a new kind of money that's entirely digital and operates independently of any central authority. It's a technological innovation that has the potential to redefine how we perceive and use money.

But it's not just about money. Cryptocurrency is part of a larger ecosystem involving blockchain technology, smart contracts, decentralized finance (DeFi), and Non-Fungible Tokens (NFTs). It's about empowering people, enabling business innovation, and creating a more inclusive financial system.

This ebook will take you on a journey into the world of cryptocurrencies. We'll start by understanding what cryptocurrency is, the technology behind it, and why it matters. Then, we'll dive into the various types of cryptocurrencies and how to buy and store them. We'll demystify the art of cryptocurrency trading and investing, and introduce you to advanced concepts like Initial Coin Offerings (ICOs), DeFi, and NFTs.

We'll also discuss the risks and challenges you'll need to navigate in the cryptocurrency world. It's not all sunshine and roses; there's a high degree of risk and volatility associated with these digital assets.

Finally, we'll gaze into the crystal ball and explore what the future might hold for cryptocurrency.

So, whether you're looking to invest in cryptocurrency or simply quench your intellectual curiosity, this book is your starting point. We hope to empower you with the knowledge you need to navigate this exciting new frontier confidently.

Let's embark on this journey together, into the heart of the digital currency revolution.

Summary of Learning Outcomes

In this comprehensive guide, readers will gain a well-rounded understanding of the world of cryptocurrencies and the underlying technologies that make them tick. Here are the key takeaways:

1. **Cryptocurrency Basics**: The reader will learn about the fundamentals of cryptocurrencies, including what they are, how they work, and why they are important.

2. **Buying and Investing**: The guide will teach readers how to get started with buying, trading, and investing in cryptocurrencies, including key strategies, risk management techniques, and how to use crypto exchanges.

3. **Cryptocurrency Management**: Readers will understand how to manage their digital assets using crypto wallets, including choosing the right wallet and securing their assets.

4. Blockchain Technology: The book dives deep into the technology that underpins cryptocurrencies, namely blockchain, explaining its functioning, significance, and potential applications.

5. Advanced Concepts: The guide provides an in-depth look at more advanced concepts like smart contracts, Decentralized Finance (DeFi), and Non-Fungible Tokens (NFTs), highlighting their role in the crypto ecosystem.

6. Regulatory Landscape: The reader will gain an understanding of the regulatory environment surrounding cryptocurrencies, how it varies across different regions, and its impact on the market.

7. Future of Cryptocurrencies: The guide concludes with a look at the potential future of cryptocurrencies, including ongoing challenges, potential developments, and impacts on various sectors.

8. Crypto Vocabulary: In the appendix, the reader will find a glossary of key terms that will help in understanding and navigating the world of cryptocurrencies more effectively.

By the end of this eBook, readers will not only have a solid foundational knowledge of cryptocurrencies but also a grasp on more complex concepts and the skills needed to actively participate in the crypto world. Whether you're a novice exploring this new field or a seasoned investor looking to deepen your knowledge, this guide provides valuable insights into the fascinating world of cryptocurrencies.

"Cryptocurrency Simplified: A Beginner's Guide to Digital Wealth"

Table of Contents

Chapter 1: What is Cryptocurrency?

Defining Cryptocurrency

Let's start at the very beginning - what exactly is a cryptocurrency? In the simplest terms, a cryptocurrency is a type of digital or virtual currency that uses cryptography for security. Unlike traditional currencies issued by central banks (like the US dollar, Euro, or Yen), cryptocurrencies operate on a technology called blockchain, which is decentralized. This means that they're not controlled by any government or single entity.

History of Cryptocurrency

While the concept of digital cash has been around since the late 1980s, with systems like DigiCash emerging, it wasn't until 2009 that the first true cryptocurrency was introduced: Bitcoin.

Bitcoin was invented by an anonymous person (or group of people) using the pseudonym Satoshi Nakamoto. The details of this new digital cash system were published in the "Bitcoin Whitepaper." Nakamoto's key innovation was solving the "double-spend" problem that plagued earlier attempts at digital currency. This problem involves a digital token being copied and spent more than once, much like if you could duplicate a dollar bill and spend it in multiple places simultaneously.

Understanding Decentralization

One of the core components of cryptocurrency is its decentralized nature. But what does that mean? In traditional financial systems, transactions are processed by a central authority, such as a bank or a credit card company. With cryptocurrencies, however, there's no need for a middleman. Instead, transactions are recorded on a distributed ledger known as a blockchain. This ledger is maintained by a network of computers, or nodes, each holding a copy of the blockchain.

Decentralization provides several advantages. It reduces the risk of a single point of failure, increases transparency, and enables peer-to-peer transactions, to name a few. It also presents an alternative to the traditional banking system for those who, for various reasons, may not have access to it.

The Role of Blockchain Technology

Blockchain technology is the backbone of cryptocurrency. A blockchain is essentially a digital ledger of transactions that is duplicated and distributed across a network of computers. These computers use a consensus algorithm to agree on the state of the ledger. Once data is recorded in a block on the blockchain, it is extremely difficult to change it, providing a high degree of security.

Blockchain technology isn't confined to the world of cryptocurrencies alone. It's being explored for various uses across industries, from supply chain to healthcare to voting systems, all thanks to its transparency, security, and efficiency.

By the end of this chapter, you should have a basic understanding of what cryptocurrencies are and why they matter. They represent not just a new form of currency, but also a new way of thinking about financial transactions and trust. As we delve deeper into the world of cryptocurrencies, you'll learn how to interact with these systems, understand their potential risks and rewards, and hopefully make informed decisions about your involvement in this space.

Chapter 2: Understanding Blockchain

What is Blockchain?

Blockchain technology is the bedrock of cryptocurrencies and is set to revolutionize various other industries as well. A blockchain is a type of distributed ledger technology, where data is stored across multiple systems worldwide in a decentralized manner. Essentially, it's a chain of blocks, where each block contains a list of transactions.

Imagine a giant spreadsheet that is duplicated and updated continuously across a network of computers. Each change in data is recorded and added as a block to this spreadsheet. This is a basic way to understand blockchain.

How Does Blockchain Work?

Every time a transaction occurs, it must be recorded in a block. Before a block can be added to the chain, however, a few things need to happen:

1. **Verification**: When a transaction is initiated, the network of computers (or nodes) begins to verify the details of the transaction. These details could include the transaction time, the parties involved, and the amount.
2. **Storage**: Once verified, the transaction's details are stored in a block. This block also contains data from other transactions, a timestamp, and an unique identifier called a cryptographic hash.
3. **Hashing**: The block is given a hash—a unique string of characters generated by a complex mathematical algorithm. Importantly, the block also contains the hash of the previous block in the chain, which forms the 'chain' of blocks.

4. **Adding to the Chain**: The newly hashed block is added to the blockchain. This updated version of the blockchain is then validated by all the nodes on the network, ensuring it's consistent and unaltered.

Once a block is added to the blockchain, altering its information becomes extremely difficult, providing a high level of security.

The Importance and Benefits of Blockchain

The primary benefits of blockchain include:

1. **Decentralization**: There's no central authority in a blockchain network, reducing the risk of central points of failure and censorship.
2. **Transparency**: Since the blockchain ledger is distributed among all participants, it offers unmatched transparency. Anyone can view the transactions on the blockchain.
3. **Security**: Changing information within a block requires re-mining not just the block in question but all subsequent blocks, which is nearly impossible due to the computational power required. This provides a high degree of security against fraud and cyber-attacks.
4. **Efficiency**: With its peer-to-peer structure, blockchain eliminates the need for middlemen in transactions, reducing costs and increasing efficiency.

Use Cases Outside of Cryptocurrency

While cryptocurrencies are the most well-known application of blockchain technology, it's being applied across various sectors, including:

- **Supply Chain Management**: Blockchain can improve traceability, transparency, and efficiency, enhancing overall supply chain operations.
- **Healthcare**: Patient records can be securely stored and shared across various providers, improving care coordination and patient outcomes.

- **Voting**: Blockchain can provide a secure and transparent platform for voting, reducing chances of fraud and enhancing trust in the process.
- **Real Estate**: From property transactions to land registries, blockchain can bring more transparency, reduce fraud, and streamline processes.

The potential uses for blockchain technology are vast and varied, and as you delve deeper into the world of cryptocurrencies, understanding blockchain will be fundamental. In the next chapter, we'll explore some of the most popular cryptocurrencies, starting with Bitcoin, the pioneer that started it all.

Chapter 3: Most Popular Cryptocurrencies

Cryptocurrencies have grown from a single, pioneering Bitcoin to over 10,000 different tokens as of 2023. With such a wide range of options, it can be challenging to navigate the landscape. In this chapter, we'll cover some of the most significant and influential cryptocurrencies in the market.

Bitcoin (BTC)

Bitcoin, often referred to as digital gold, is the first and most widely recognized cryptocurrency. Invented by the pseudonymous Satoshi Nakamoto, Bitcoin is a peer-to-peer digital currency that allows users to send and receive money over the internet without the need for a centralized authority. Bitcoin's supply is capped at 21 million coins, a feature that has largely contributed to its value as it creates scarcity.

Ethereum (ETH)

Ethereum, created by Vitalik Buterin, is not just a cryptocurrency—it's a platform for creating decentralized applications (dApps) using smart contracts. A smart contract is a self-executing contract where the terms are written directly into code, ensuring trust between parties. Ethereum's native currency is Ether (ETH), used to facilitate transactions on the network and incentivize developers. Ethereum has pioneered the concept of a blockchain beyond simply transferring value, making it one of the most important cryptocurrencies and blockchain projects.

Binance Coin (BNB)

Binance Coin is the native cryptocurrency of the Binance exchange, one of the largest cryptocurrency exchanges in the world. Initially created on the Ethereum network, BNB now operates on the Binance Smart Chain, a blockchain network built for running smart contract-based applications. BNB can be used to pay for fees on the Binance platform, participate in token sales, and more.

Cardano (ADA)

Cardano, developed by a team led by Ethereum's co-founder Charles Hoskinson, aims to be a "third generation blockchain," addressing the issues of scalability, interoperability, and sustainability that have been problematic for earlier blockchains. Cardano's native currency, ADA, is named after Ada Lovelace, a 19th-century mathematician recognized as the first computer programmer.

Other Notable Cryptocurrencies

There are numerous other cryptocurrencies worth mentioning, including:

- **Ripple (XRP)**: Designed for large financial institutions rather than individual users, Ripple provides a system for rapid, low-fee international money transfers.
- **Polkadot (DOT)**: Created by another Ethereum co-founder, Dr. Gavin Wood, Polkadot aims to enable different blockchains to operate together seamlessly.
- **Chainlink (LINK)**: A decentralized oracle network that enables smart contracts to securely interact with real-world data and external APIs.

- **Dogecoin (DOGE)**: Originally created as a meme cryptocurrency, Dogecoin has gained significant popularity and community support.

While the cryptocurrencies listed here are among the most popular and established, the crypto landscape is dynamic and rapidly evolving. New projects continue to emerge, and the value and relevance of existing ones can fluctuate dramatically. Therefore, it's crucial to continuously learn, research, and stay updated in this field. In the next chapter, we'll take a closer look at how to buy, sell, and store these digital assets safely.

Chapter 4: How to Buy and Store Cryptocurrencies

Now that we have a basic understanding of what cryptocurrencies are and a familiarity with the most popular ones, let's delve into how you can buy and store these digital assets.

Introduction to Exchanges

Cryptocurrency exchanges are platforms where you can buy, sell, and sometimes store cryptocurrencies. These exchanges often operate similarly to stock exchanges, allowing users to buy and sell assets at market prices, with the platform taking a small fee from each transaction. Here are a few notable ones:

- **Coinbase**: One of the most user-friendly exchanges, perfect for beginners. It supports a variety of cryptocurrencies and offers educational content for beginners.
- **Binance**: This is one of the largest and most well-known exchanges globally. Binance offers a wide range of cryptocurrencies and additional features like futures trading and staking.
- **Kraken**: Known for its security features and robust platform, Kraken also offers a wide variety of cryptocurrencies.
- **Gemini**: Founded by the Winklevoss twins, Gemini is a US-based exchange known for its strong regulatory compliance and security features.

When choosing an exchange, consider factors such as security, user interface, supported cryptocurrencies, fees, and customer support.

How to Buy Cryptocurrencies

Here's a basic step-by-step guide on how to buy cryptocurrencies:

1. **Create an Account**: Choose your preferred exchange and sign up for an account. This usually involves providing some personal information and verifying your identity.
2. **Secure Your Account**: Enable two-factor authentication (2FA) to add an extra layer of security to your account.
3. **Deposit Funds**: You can deposit funds into your exchange account using various methods, such as bank transfer, credit/debit card, or even transferring cryptocurrency from another wallet.
4. **Buy Cryptocurrency**: Navigate to the market for the cryptocurrency you wish to purchase, enter the amount you want to buy, and execute the transaction.
5. **Confirm Transaction**: Check your wallet on the exchange to ensure the purchased cryptocurrency is there.

Wallets and Their Importance

Once you buy cryptocurrencies, you need to store them securely. This is where cryptocurrency wallets come in. They store the private keys required to access your cryptocurrency on the blockchain. There are various types of wallets:

- **Online Wallets**: These are wallets run on the cloud. They are accessible from any device and easy to use. However, they are also more vulnerable to hacking attempts and scams.
- **Mobile Wallets**: These are apps on your phone. They are convenient, especially for retail payments, but they could be vulnerable if your phone is compromised.
- **Desktop Wallets**: Downloaded and installed on a PC or laptop, these wallets offer a good balance of convenience and security.

- **Hardware Wallets**: These are the most secure option. They are physical devices, similar to a USB stick, that store your private keys offline.
- **Paper Wallets**: This involves printing your private keys on a piece of paper and storing it in a secure place. It's secure but can be complicated for beginners.

Importance of Private Keys and Security

Your private key is like a digital signature; it's proof that you own your digital assets. If you lose it or it gets stolen, you lose access to your cryptocurrency.

Here are some security measures to keep in mind:

- Never share your private keys with anyone.
- Always enable two-factor authentication.
- Use hardware wallets for storing large amounts of cryptocurrencies.
- Keep your software up to date.
- Be wary of phishing scams.

In the next chapter, we will delve deeper into trading and investing in cryptocurrencies, which are different from just buying and holding them.

Chapter 5: Trading and Investing in Cryptocurrencies

Entering the world of cryptocurrency can feel like stepping into an alien landscape filled with strange terms and complex processes. Yet, with some basic knowledge, you can navigate this landscape successfully. This chapter will delve into the basics of trading and investing in cryptocurrencies.

Investing vs. Trading

The first distinction to understand is the difference between trading and investing:

1. **Investing** is a long-term approach. When you invest in cryptocurrencies, you're buying a cryptocurrency with the belief that its value will increase over time. This method typically involves thorough research and a strong belief in the project's future.
2. **Trading** is a short-term approach. Traders aim to take advantage of the volatility of the crypto market to profit from short-term price changes. This requires a deep understanding of market trends and often involves complex tools and strategies.

Basic Trading Concepts

To get started with trading, it's important to understand a few key concepts:

1. **Order Book**: This is a list of the buy and sell orders for a particular cryptocurrency. It gives traders an idea of the supply and demand for that coin.
2. **Market Orders**: This is an order to buy or sell a coin immediately at the best available price.
3. **Limit Orders**: This is an order to buy or sell a coin at a specific price. The order will only be executed when the market price matches the limit price.
4. **Stop-Loss Orders**: This is a protective measure that triggers a sale when a certain price level is reached, preventing further losses.

Steps to Start Trading

1. **Choose a Trading Platform**: First, you need a platform to trade on. This could be a cryptocurrency exchange like Binance or Coinbase, or a platform focused on trading, like MetaTrader 4.
2. **Develop a Trading Strategy**: Are you planning to day trade (opening and closing positions within a single day) or swing trade (holding positions over several days)? What indicators will you use to decide when to buy and sell?
3. **Start Small**: Trading involves a higher risk than investing, especially for beginners. Start with a small amount that you're willing to lose and practice your strategy.

4. **Analyze and Adjust**: As you gain experience, continually analyze your trades and adjust your strategy as needed.

Investing in Cryptocurrencies

When it comes to investing in cryptocurrencies, here are some steps to follow:

1. **Research**: Look into the project's white paper, the team behind it, its use case, and any news or developments related to it.
2. **Diversify**: Don't put all your eggs in one basket. Spread your investments across different cryptocurrencies to mitigate risk.
3. **Be Patient**: Investing is a long-term game. Hasty decisions can lead to losses, so it's crucial to be patient and avoid panic selling.
4. **Stay Updated**: Keep up with news and updates about your investments. This can inform you of any changes that might influence your investment's long-term value.

Remember, both trading and investing come with the risk of losing your capital. It's important to only invest money you can afford to lose. Additionally, constant education is key to success in the ever-evolving world of cryptocurrencies.

In the next chapter, we will delve into the world of blockchain technology, smart contracts, and Decentralized Finance (DeFi) - more complex but increasingly important areas of the cryptocurrency space.

Chapter 6: Delving Deeper: Blockchain Technology, Smart Contracts, and DeFi

In the world of cryptocurrencies, trading and investing are just the tip of the iceberg. Beneath the surface lies a complex ecosystem built on innovative technologies, including blockchain, smart contracts, and a fast-evolving field called Decentralized Finance (DeFi).

Understanding Blockchain Technology

A blockchain is essentially a decentralized ledger of all transactions across a peer-to-peer network. Using this technology, participants can confirm transactions without the need for a central clearing authority. Here's how it works:

1. **Transaction**: Whenever a transaction occurs, it is grouped together in a block with other transactions that have happened in the same time frame.
2. **Verification**: These transactions are then verified by miners (people using powerful computers to solve complex mathematical problems) across the network.
3. **Adding to the Chain**: Once verified, the block of transactions is added to the existing blockchain, which is permanent and unalterable.

The beauty of blockchain is that it promotes transparency and reduces the risk of fraud, as each participant has access to the same ledger of transactions.

Smart Contracts and Ethereum

Smart contracts are self-executing contracts with the terms of the agreement directly written into code. They automatically execute transactions when predefined conditions are met, reducing the need for intermediaries and increasing efficiency.

Ethereum is a decentralized, open-source blockchain that was designed specifically to facilitate smart contracts. While Bitcoin was designed primarily as a digital currency, Ethereum has expanded the potential applications of blockchain technology.

Decentralized Finance (DeFi)

Decentralized Finance, or DeFi, refers to the use of blockchain, cryptocurrencies, smart contracts, and decentralized applications (dApps) to recreate and improve upon traditional financial systems.

Here's a quick overview of some common DeFi applications:

- **Decentralized Exchanges (DEXs)**: These platforms allow users to trade cryptocurrencies directly with one another, eliminating the need for an intermediary.
- **Lending Platforms**: These platforms allow users to lend and borrow cryptocurrencies directly with each other, often earning interest on deposits.
- **Stablecoins**: These are cryptocurrencies designed to minimize volatility by pegging their value to an external reference, such as the US dollar.
- **Yield Farming and Liquidity Mining**: These are strategies where users lock up their cryptocurrencies in a DeFi protocol to earn rewards.

While DeFi offers exciting opportunities, it's important to remember that it's still a relatively new and unregulated field, with its own unique risks. Always do your own research and exercise caution when interacting with DeFi platforms.

In the next chapter, we will explore another burgeoning field within the crypto world - Non-Fungible Tokens (NFTs), which have opened up new possibilities in the worlds of art, entertainment, and beyond.

Chapter 7: Exploring Non-Fungible Tokens (NFTs)

The world of cryptocurrencies extends beyond decentralized finance. A rapidly emerging sector in the crypto space is the market for Non-Fungible Tokens, or NFTs, a unique type of digital asset.

Understanding NFTs

Non-Fungible Tokens (NFTs) are unique digital assets verified using blockchain technology, which provides proof of ownership and authenticity. Unlike cryptocurrencies like Bitcoin or Ethereum, which are fungible and can be exchanged on a like-for-like basis, each NFT has unique properties and can't be exchanged on a like-for-like basis. In other words, they are digital collectibles.

NFTs can represent ownership or proof of authenticity for a wide variety of assets, both digital and physical. They've been used for digital art, music, virtual real estate in digital worlds, domain names, and more.

Why Do NFTs Matter?

NFTs have the potential to revolutionize many industries by solving problems related to ownership and provenance. For artists and creators, NFTs offer a way to sell their work directly to consumers without the need for intermediaries. Moreover, through "smart contracts", artists can receive royalties every time their work is resold, which was not possible before.

For collectors, NFTs provide verifiable proof of ownership, a crucial factor in the world of collectibles. They also enable the ownership of digital assets, expanding the realm of collectibles to digital art, virtual goods, and more.

Buying and Selling NFTs

Buying and selling NFTs is generally done on specialized platforms. Some of the most popular NFT marketplaces include OpenSea, Rarible, and NBA Top Shot. These platforms allow creators to mint (create) NFTs and list them for sale, while collectors can browse, buy, and resell NFTs.

When buying NFTs, it's important to consider the reputation of the seller, the rarity and demand for the NFT, and the terms of the smart contract attached to it. As with any investment, it's crucial to do thorough research.

The Future of NFTs

The NFT market is still in its early stages, and it's hard to predict exactly how it will evolve. However, the potential applications of NFTs are vast. They could change the way we own and trade assets, creating new opportunities for creators, collectors, investors, and businesses.

However, as exciting as NFTs are, they come with their own set of risks, including price volatility, lack of regulatory oversight, and potential copyright issues. So, if you're planning to get involved with NFTs, be sure to understand what you're buying and the risks involved.

In the next chapter, we will address how governments around the world are reacting to cryptocurrencies and the impacts these reactions are having on the market. It's crucial to understand the regulatory environment when dealing with cryptocurrencies.

Chapter 8: Navigating the Regulatory Landscape of Cryptocurrencies

As the popularity and impact of cryptocurrencies have grown, so too has the attention from government regulators around the world. The response has been mixed, with some countries embracing the innovation while others have raised concerns about security, economic stability, and criminal activity.

Regulation in Various Countries

Different countries have responded to cryptocurrencies in different ways:

1. **United States**: The regulatory landscape in the U.S. is complex and fragmented, with various federal and state agencies claiming jurisdiction over different aspects of crypto activity. The Securities and Exchange Commission (SEC) oversees securities (including certain ICOs), while the Commodity Futures Trading Commission (CFTC) regulates commodity futures and swaps. The IRS treats cryptocurrencies as property for tax purposes.

2. **European Union**: The EU has not adopted a uniform approach to cryptocurrency regulation, leaving member states to develop their own guidelines. However, the EU has expressed interest in establishing a comprehensive regulatory framework to protect investors and mitigate risks.
3. **China**: China has taken a strict approach, banning Initial Coin Offerings (ICOs) and crypto exchanges. The government has recently reiterated its ban on cryptocurrency trading and has taken steps to crack down on mining activities.
4. **Japan**: Japan has been more embracing, officially recognizing cryptocurrencies as legal property and requiring cryptocurrency exchanges to register with the government.

Impacts of Regulation

Regulation can have significant impacts on the cryptocurrency market:

- **Legitimacy**: Proper regulation can lend legitimacy to cryptocurrencies, attracting more participation from institutional investors and traditional finance.
- **Investor Protection**: Regulatory oversight can protect investors from fraud and market manipulation, which have been issues in the largely unregulated crypto market.
- **Market Stability**: By implementing clear guidelines and oversight, regulators can help reduce the volatility and risk associated with the crypto market.

Navigating the Regulatory Landscape

As an individual in the cryptocurrency space, it's important to stay informed about the regulatory environment. Here are a few tips:

1. **Understand Your Local Laws**: Regulatory approaches can vary significantly from country to country, and even state to state. Be sure to understand the laws and regulations in your area.

2. **Stay Informed**: The regulatory environment is rapidly evolving. Keep up with news and updates to understand how changes may affect your investments.
3. **Consider Tax Implications**: In many jurisdictions, cryptocurrencies are subject to taxes. Be sure you understand your tax obligations.
4. **Beware of Fraud**: While regulation can help curb fraudulent activity, scams are still common in the crypto space. Always do your own research and be cautious.

Regulation is an essential part of the maturation of the cryptocurrency market. While it can bring challenges, it also brings the potential for greater stability and acceptance. In our final chapter, we'll look at the future of cryptocurrencies and the potential paths this exciting technology could take.

Chapter 9: The Future of Cryptocurrencies: What Lies Ahead?

As we draw close to the end of this guide, it's time to look towards the horizon and explore what the future might hold for cryptocurrencies. Cryptocurrencies, born from technological innovation, are continually evolving, with new use cases, platforms, and developments emerging every day.

Continuous Technological Innovation

One of the defining characteristics of cryptocurrencies is the relentless pace of innovation. We have already witnessed this with the emergence of smart contracts, DeFi, and NFTs. The technology that underpins cryptocurrencies – blockchain – has potential applications far beyond just digital money. In the coming years, we can expect to see further evolution and potentially even more transformative use cases emerging.

Growing Institutional Adoption

In the past, cryptocurrencies were primarily the realm of individual tech enthusiasts and investors. However, this has been changing. We are seeing an increasing number of businesses, financial institutions, and even governments taking an interest in cryptocurrencies. This trend could lead to wider acceptance, more use cases, and greater stability in the market.

Regulatory Developments

As discussed in Chapter 8, regulation is a significant factor influencing the future of cryptocurrencies. A regulatory crackdown could pose challenges, while clear and supportive regulation could spur further growth and adoption. The way governments around the world approach this challenge will be crucial.

Challenges Ahead

While the future of cryptocurrencies is promising, it's important not to overlook the potential challenges:

- **Scalability**: As more people use cryptocurrencies, networks can become congested, leading to slower transactions and higher fees.
- **Security**: While blockchain technology is inherently secure, the platforms and services built on top of it can be vulnerable to hacks.
- **Environmental Impact**: The energy consumption of some cryptocurrencies, particularly those that use proof-of-work consensus mechanisms like Bitcoin, has been a subject of concern.

Conclusion

As we've seen throughout this guide, cryptocurrencies are more than just a form of digital money – they represent a new way of building and interacting with financial and digital services. From understanding the basics of what cryptocurrencies are, how to trade and invest in them, and the more advanced concepts of DeFi, NFTs, and regulatory landscapes, you now have a foundational knowledge of this complex and exciting field.

The future of cryptocurrencies is still being written, and there will undoubtedly be many twists and turns on the path ahead. However, one thing seems certain – cryptocurrencies are here to stay, and they have the potential to change the world in profound ways. By continuing to learn and stay engaged with cryptocurrencies, you are part of this exciting journey. Good luck, and happy crypto adventures!

Appendix: Glossary of Key Cryptocurrency Terms

1. **Address**: A string of alphanumeric characters that is used to receive cryptocurrencies.
2. **Altcoin**: Any cryptocurrency other than Bitcoin.
3. **Blockchain**: A decentralized ledger of all transactions across a peer-to-peer network.
4. **Bitcoin**: The first decentralized cryptocurrency, created in 2009 by an individual or group of individuals using the pseudonym Satoshi Nakamoto.
5. **Cold Storage**: A security measure for storing cryptocurrencies offline to prevent unauthorized access.
6. **Crypto Wallet**: A digital wallet where you can store, send, and receive cryptocurrencies.
7. **Decentralized Finance (DeFi)**: The use of blockchain, cryptocurrencies, smart contracts, and decentralized applications (dApps) to recreate and improve upon traditional financial systems.
8. **Decentralized Exchange (DEX)**: A platform that allows users to trade cryptocurrencies directly with one another without an intermediary.
9. **Fiat**: Government-issued money, such as USD, EUR, or JPY.
10. **Fungible**: Something that can be replaced by another identical item; mutually interchangeable.
11. **Hard Fork**: A type of protocol upgrade that is not backward-compatible. This means that all network participants must upgrade their software to the new version of the protocol.
12. **Hash**: A function that converts an input of letters and numbers into an encrypted output of a fixed length.

13. **Initial Coin Offering (ICO)**: A type of crowdfunding using cryptocurrencies.
14. **Mining**: The process of validating new transactions and recording them on a blockchain.

1. **Non-Fungible Token (NFT)**: A type of digital asset that represents ownership or proof of authenticity for a unique item or piece of content.
2. **Private Key**: A string of data that allows you to access the tokens in a specific wallet.
3. **Public Key**: A string of data that is publicly available and allows others to send you cryptocurrency.
4. **Satoshi**: The smallest unit of Bitcoin, equivalent to 100 millionth of a Bitcoin.
5. **Smart Contract**: A self-executing contract with the terms of the agreement directly written into code.
6. **Stablecoin**: A type of cryptocurrency designed to minimize volatility by pegging its value to an external reference, such as the US dollar.
7. **Token**: A digital asset that represents a particular asset or utility.
8. **Wallet**: A digital or physical tool that allows an individual to store and manage their cryptocurrency.